ABRAHAM JOSHUA HESCHEL

MAKERS OF CONTEMPORARY THEOLOGY

MAKERS OF CONTEMPORARY THEOLOGY

ABRAHAM JOSHUA HESCHEL

by

BYRON L. SHERWIN

John Knox Press
ATLANTA

Library of Congress Cataloging in Publication Data

Sherwin, Byron L
    Abraham Joshua Heschel.

    (Makers of contemporary theology)
    Includes bibliographical references.
    1. Heschel, Abraham Joshua, 1907–1972.
BM755.H37S49   296'.3'0924   78–71051
ISBN 0–8042–0466–7

© copyright John Knox Press 1979

Printed in the United States of America
Atlanta, Georgia

For Elliott:

A little book,
for my little brother

Contents

Preface

THE following story is told about the medieval Christian philosopher, Alan of Lille.

Alan was once on his way to deliver a lecture on the mystery of the Trinity at the University of Paris. En route, he happened to stop at the bank of a river. A small boy had dug a hole in the sand near the river and was filling it with water he had carried from the river in a small bucket.

"What are you doing?" Alan asked him.

"I am trying to empty all of the water of the river into the hole I have dug," answered the boy.

Alan walked on, reflecting upon the futile efforts of the small boy. Only then did Alan realize that his own attempt to compress the complexities of the doctrine of the Trinity into a single lecture was equally as futile. Similarly, to compress the complexities of Abraham Joshua Heschel's life and thought into the confines of a small book is a difficult, if not an impossible task. We can only survey the surface, and not plumb the depths. Nevertheless, if the reader is stimulated by the following discussion to read Heschel's works, the author rests content. If those who have read Heschel's works find a new level of understanding in the following pages, then the writer's effort to empty the water of the river of Heschel's massive flow of ideas into this small book has not been futile.

I

Life

ABRAHAM JOSHUA HESCHEL was a jewel from God's treasure chest. When he departed life on December 23, 1972, God lost an agent of his compassion; Jewish scholarship lost one of its most original, erudite, and penetrating minds; victims of social injustice and moral scandal lost a champion; students lost a teacher; and disciples lost a master. His life was a symphony of gracious deeds and sublime thoughts. Both in word and deed, he scored singular success in relating yesterday's wisdom to today's perplexities. He was the rabbi who could elucidate the fine points of classical Judaica, the philosopher able to analyze abstruse medieval concepts and the author who mastered the art of writing classics. There are many human beings who aspire to scholarship and there are many scholars who aspire to be human beings, but these aspirations are rarely wedded in a single person. Abraham Heschel was such a person.

Heschel was born in Warsaw in 1907, a prince amongst Hasidim.[1] In his late teens, already ordained a rabbi, the precocious prodigy left the confines of Warsaw to study philosophy at the University of Berlin. In 1933 he published his first book, a slim volume of Yiddish poems, and in 1936 his doctoral dissertation on the prophets of Israel. This extraordinary treatise revolutionized contemporary understanding of prophecy. When an expanded English version appeared in 1962, it was eagerly appropriated by universities and seminaries as a textbook for Biblical studies.

Already established as a Biblical scholar, the young Heschel immersed himself in medieval Jewish philosophy. He wrote a series of studies on the unique contributions to the history of philosophy by the eleventh century poet and philosopher, Solomon ibn Gabirol, who so significantly influenced Christian scholasticism. In 1935, on the eight-hundredth anniversary of Maimonides' birth, Heschel authored an existential biography of Maimonides in a flowing German prose.[2] In 1937 he wrote a slender volume on Don Isaac Abravanel. This monograph about this sixteenth century Jewish scholar-statesman who attained high honors at the Spanish and Portuguese courts and enriched the culture of his native land, but who was expelled with his people from Iberia, must have touched the hearts of German Jews fleeing from Hitler's hordes.

In Germany Heschel began to produce students as well as books. In 1932 he was appointed an instructor in Talmud, another field of his wide expertise, at the prestigious *Hochschule für die Wissenschaft des Judentums* (Academy for Jewish Studies), of which he was an alumnus. When Martin Buber left Germany for Palestine, he chose Heschel as his successor at the prominent *Jüdisches Lehrhaus* in Frankfurt. In 1938, together with all Jews holding Polish passports, Heschel was arrested and deported from Germany, leaving behind many manuscripts, friends, and hopes. He returned to Warsaw where he taught briefly. Six weeks before the *blitzkrieg*, Heschel departed for London where he founded the Institute for Adult Jewish Studies. In 1940 he was called to America by the Hebrew Union College. Though he arrived in the United States knowing no English, within a few years he developed a flowing, flawless English style. Heschel continued his studies in medieval philosophy, publishing a masterful work in 1942 on the philosophy of Saadia Gaon to commemorate the thousandth anniversary of the latter's death.[3] In 1945 he expanded his earlier work on Maimonides by publishing a Hebrew essay on Maimonides' secret quest for prophecy. By this time Heschel had accepted a position at The Jewish Theological Seminary of America, a post he retained until his death twenty-seven years later.

Heschel's continuing effort to emphasize the meaningfulness of Judaism's message for modern man is demonstrated by his masterful interpretation of the Jewish Sabbath, *The Sabbath*, published in 1950 and by his challenging study on Jewish prayer, *Man's Quest for God*, published in 1954. *The Earth Is the Lord's*, based upon a Yiddish address delivered in 1946, is Heschel's moving eulogy to the destroyed Jewish communities of Eastern Europe. The Rabbi of Kotsk, the subject of Heschel's final work, had said: "There are three ways to assuage sorrow: one is to cry, one is to be silent, and one is to turn sorrow into song." Heschel's volume, written in a unique poetic prose, is a song for that which was lost. *Man Is Not Alone*, his philosophy of religion, perceives religion as human piety responding to the ineffable marvel of existence. It offers a refreshing and compelling alternative to the prevalent over-systematized and over-secularized philosophies of religion. *God in Search of Man*, Heschel's philosophy of Judaism, perceives Judaism as being grounded in God's search for human righteousness rather than in the fulfillment of a human psychological need. Revelation, through which God reaches people and communicates his plan for human fulfillment, becomes a central postulate in Heschel's thinking. A formulation of prophetic revelation forms the core both of *God in Search of Man* and of his work on the prophets. The rabbinic understanding of revelation is also the central theme of the second volume of Heschel's massive Hebrew work, *The Theology of Ancient Judaism*.

A poignant combination of a poetic outcry and a philosophically cogent polemic against philosophies of hopelessness and policies which encourage dehumanization, became still another book, *Who Is Man?* In 1967, when Jews throughout the world struggled to verbalize a blessing of gratitude for the State of Israel while simultaneously striving to respond cogently to anti-Zionist rhetoric, it was Abraham Heschel who best managed to articulate the thoughts of world Jewry. His *Israel: Echo of Eternity* is both a tender serenade to Jerusalem and a powerful polemic against apathy and hostility toward Israel.

During the 1950s and 60s, the scion of Hasidic sages produced a series of Hebrew and Yiddish studies on early Hasidic masters. His last published works deal with the enigmatic Rabbi Mendel of Kotsk. In a definitive two-volume Yiddish study, Heschel scrutinizes the personality and ideas of this militant, uncompromising Hasidic master who attempted to engender a reformation within Hasidism by demanding ruthless honesty and authenticity while disparaging mediocrity and mendacity. In *A Passion for Truth*, Heschel compares Rabbi Mendel of Kotsk with Søren Kierkegaard, considered by many the father of existentialism, and makes available to the English reader the essential ideas of his huge Yiddish tome. While some writers are content to author a single magnum opus in a single language, Heschel produced three, each in a different language: *God in Search of Man* in English, *The Theology of Ancient Judaism* in Hebrew, and *Kotsk: The Struggle for Integrity* in Yiddish. Thus, in forty years, despite having been geographically transplanted a number of times, notwithstanding heavy teaching and lecturing loads, Abraham Heschel produced in four languages over twenty volumes and scores of scholarly treatises and essays, each a landmark in itself.

To have excelled as a scholar, teacher, and author would have sufficed most men, but not Abraham Heschel. Like Rabbi Mendel of Kotsk, he remained secluded to do his careful and intricate scholarly work. But like the founder of Hasidism, the Baal Shem Tov, he went directly to people and talked to them about concrete issues in strikingly direct terms. Heschel preferred sincerity and authenticity to popularity, and he told people exactly what he thought. Like Abraham of old, he believed in smashing idols rather than in compromising truth.

Heschel admonished the General Assembly of the Council of Jewish Federations and Welfare Funds that its members and supporters "are often concerned with digits" while the community is in "spiritual distress." He reminded those who measure religious commitment by the amount of money donated: "An old Jewish principle proclaims, 'The world stands on three pillars: on learning, on worship and on charity' (*Aboth* 1:2). We are not going to invite a friend to sit on a tripod, a stool designed to have three legs, when two legs are missing."[4]

He talked to Catholics and chastised them for having a Roman Catholic church next to Auschwitz which offered communion to the officers of the camp who killed thousands of people each day.[5]

At an annual convention of the American Medical Association, he indicated, "The patient is haunted with fear, but some doctors are in a hurry, and above all, impatient. They have something in common with God; they cannot be easily reached, not even at the golf course."[6]

Heschel spoke to clergymen and religious educators about the separation of church and God. He identified the *spiritual* absenteeism which characterizes much of American religious life. According to Heschel, the synagogues and the churches suffer from an identical malady—a severe cold. They presume to think that spiritual problems can be solved by administrative techniques.

In the mid-1960s when the "God is dead" theology was the rage, Heschel denounced it as a "fad." Humanity might be dead, the human conscience may have become an unconscious fossil, but God, for Heschel, is very much alive. Referring to the "theologians" of the "God is dead" tendency, Heschel wrote: "Some of us are like patients in the state of final agony—who scream in delirium: the doctor is dead, the doctor is dead."[7]

What has been said of the Christian theologian, Karl Barth, may also be said of Abraham Heschel—his words and his literary works are like a bomb which has exploded in the playgrounds of the theologians.

Not complacent with books and with words, Abraham Heschel responded to the needs of the times also with deeds. In 1942, when Heschel, newly arrived from a doomed Jewish world, approached leaders of American Jewry to intercede to help save European Jewry, they responded with hostility or apathy. Twenty years later, when he sought to awaken organized

Jewry to the plight of the Russian Jews, he was greeted with equal impassivity. By the time the leaders in the 40s responded, it was too late. But in the 60s, the Jewish community eventually mobilized in response to his original call.

When President Eisenhower convened the White House Conference on Children and Youth in 1960, it was Heschel's paper which he found so impressive as to invite him to return the following year to present a statement at the White House Conference on Aging. These and others of Heschel's views on social issues form a volume entitled *The Insecurity of Freedom*.

When Pope John decided that the Catholic Church should rethink its centuries-old view of Judaism and the Jew, it was Abraham Heschel whom the Pontiff saw. His audiences with Pope John and later with Pope Paul ultimately resulted in the Ecumenical Council's *Schema on the Jews*, in which the Church conceded that for two thousand years, its doctrine concerning the Jews had been a mistake.

In 1965, despite condemnation and opposition from many quarters, Heschel insightfully and courageously denounced the war in Vietnam as a "moral outrage." To his fellow clergymen, Heschel cajoled: "To speak about God and remain silent on Vietnam is blasphemous."

It was largely because of Heschel's efforts that Martin Luther King actively joined the anti-war movement. To be sure, King's efforts in this regard were challenged, even within the black community. When Heschel was once challenged with the query: "What right does King have to speak out against the war in Vietnam; should he not concentrate only on civil rights?" Heschel retorted: "Certainly, the winner of the Nobel Prize for peace has the right to speak out against war and for peace."

A co-founder of Clergy and Laymen Concerned About Vietnam, Heschel persisted in his anti-war efforts during the Johnson and Nixon years. Not a dreamer detached from awareness of the *realpolitik*, Heschel understood that "the problems are complex: power is involved, industry is involved, trade is involved." Nevertheless, he felt compelled to ask: "But what about life itself? What about humanity itself?"[8] For Heschel, moral responsibility cannot be surrendered by proxy. In his words, "We must continue to remind ourselves that all are involved in what some are doing. Some are guilty, all are responsible."[9]

According to Heschel, matters of life and death, of peace and war, are matters too serious to be left to "a few individuals in Washington." To delegate "our conscience to a few diplomats and generals," is, for Heschel, "a very, very grave sin."[10]

During the last few months of Heschel's life, the American people were in the process of choosing a president. Many Jewish leaders openly supported Richard Nixon because of his strong support of the State of Israel. Heschel's intuitive distrust of President Nixon, reinforced by the persistence of the Vietnam War during Nixon's first term, reluctantly convinced Heschel to enter partisan politics by supporting the presidential candidacy of George McGovern. Virtually ostracized by Jewish leaders and rabbinic colleagues for this stance, Heschel's last few months were isolated and lonely ones. Long before the Watergate hearings, Heschel denounced the corruption of the Nixon administration. In a letter to rabbinic colleagues, written only weeks before election day, Heschel stated that which most Americans would come to realize in the months following his death:[11]

If the prophets Isaiah and Amos were to appear in our midst, would they accept the corruption in high places, the indifferent way in which the sick, the poor, and the old are treated? Would they condone the indifference to gun control legislation that has allowed some of the finest of our national leaders to be shot dead? Would not our prophets be standing with those who protest against the war in Vietnam, the decay of our cities, the hypocrisy and falsehood that surround our present administration, even at the highest level?. . .By word and by deed, Senator McGovern is committed to the idea that "setting the moral tone of this nation is the most serious responsibility of the President." Regrettably, the same cannot be said of Mr. Nixon.

Abraham Heschel was a man of his times, ahead of his times. Drawing upon the wisdom of the past, he provided spiritual therapy for the present. The readers of his works will find them evocative as well as informative. His poetic images not only shine; they burn. They sear our soul with the urgency with which God seeks man.

Heschel's writings provide the reader with a journey into the realm of ideas as well as a voyage to distant lands and past ages. The reader will meet many provocative minds; he will encounter many challenging ideas. However, he or she will also have the chance to share the insights of the author's soul. In so doing, the reader will encounter a noble soul, a profound intellect, and a wise guide. In plotting the journey of Heschel's soul throughout his works, in reading Heschel's "journal of a soul," one's own life can only become immeasurably enriched.

2
Thought

HESCHEL'S biography is intertwined with his bibliography; his deeds emanated from his ideas. His theological assumptions were the coal which generated the fire of his words and of his actions. To understand his involvement in social action and his commitment to "practical theology," one must perceive their underlying conceptual foundation.

Heschel was not a systematic theologian. Therefore, to offer a systematic and analytic presentation of his thought would deform its essence. Rather, we shall identify and discuss a number of themes central to his thinking which would prove helpful in unlocking the doors to the massive theological edifice which Heschel constructed. The first of these themes, which demonstrates the link between Heschel's thinking and his living, between his metaphysical speculation and his moral dedication, is the quest for "self-understanding."

Self-Understanding

Abraham Joshua Heschel's name was not his own. He inherited it from his ancestor, a Hasidic master, known as the rabbi of Apt (a town in Poland). According to Hasidic legend, the rabbi of Apt believed in the transmigration of souls. He therefore taught that it is important for one to know who one once was, in order for one to understand who one presently is.

The doctrine of transmigration of souls contains a profound religious truth. For one to know oneself, one must seek to understand one's past, one's heritage, the religious tradition from which one emerges. An essential key to comprehending the life and thought of Abraham Heschel is therefore contained in his namesake's belief that the human soul is not the product of *creatio ex nihilo*. The human soul is born with a past. The task of religious philosophy is to make the insights of the past compatible with the moral and religious problems of the present. The religious endeavor must be to make our history compatible with our destiny. While the religious philosopher must aspire to become an ancestor, he must first qualify to become an heir.

According to Heschel, the crisis of modern man derives from his tendency to understand himself as a *Ding an sich*, as a thing in himself, living in the present, divorced from the wisdom of the past. As such, man cannot understand himself. The human being, cut off from God and from the insights of his tradition, is a torso without a head, a body without a soul, a tree without roots.

For Heschel, one must aim to achieve "radical self-understanding." He uses the word "radical" in the literal sense meaning "roots." Modern secular man seeks self-understanding without examining his roots. Following Jewish mystical tradition, Heschel insists that the human being is like an upright tree with roots above. Without exploring his roots in the divine-human encounter as understood by religious tradition, the human quest for self-understanding becomes a dead end.

In his work *The Earth Is the Lord's*, Heschel characterizes modern man's problem by telling this story:

> Once there was a schoolboy who would be in great distress every morning when he awoke, having forgotten where he put away his clothes, and his books the night before. One evening, however, he arrived at a solution to his problem. Before going to bed, he made a list of where everything was: "the suit is on the chair, the hat is in the closet, the books are on the desk, the shoes are under the chair and I am in the bed." The next morning he found everything on the list except the last item. When he looked for himself in the bed—he discovered that he could find everything—except himself.[12]

Both Heschel's personal life and his scholarly works may be understood as a lifelong quest for self-understanding. This search is predicated upon the assumption that the wisdom of the past can elucidate the perplexities of the present. Following the medievals, Heschel insisted that the quest ends only with death. The human being is always developing, always growing. Only God can say "I am that I am." God *is*, while the human being is always *becoming*.

What Heschel wrote in 1942 about the tenth-century Jewish philosopher Saadya Gaon, was true of himself:

> The wisdom of philosophers is not a commodity that can be produced on demand. Their books are not responsa. We should not regard them as mirrors, reflecting other people's problems, but rather as windows, allowing us to view the author's soul. Philosophers do not expend their power and passion unless they themselves are affected, originally or vicariously. The soul only communes with itself when the heart is stirred.[13]

Following Heschel's own suggestion, one may view his writings as windows to his soul. This is true of his works about historical personalities as well as those expressing his own views, and of his scholarly as well as of his popular work. For Heschel, scholarship is more than a parlor game. Academics is not an end in itself, but a means to an end. In his last book, *A Passion for Truth*, Heschel asks: "What purpose was served in knowing the sacred text if one could not understand oneself?"[14] For Heschel, communion with the wisdom of the past must have personal and existential implications. The function of scholarship, for Heschel, must ultimately aim not at aesthetic pleasure or intellectual satisfaction. It must be part of an ongoing quest for self-understanding and for the enrichment of one's inner life.

In one of his books Heschel tells of a scholar who came to a certain Hasidic master. The master asked the scholar, "What have you done all your life?" To which the scholar answered,

"I have already gone through the entire Talmud three times."
To which the master replied, "Yes, but how much of the Talmud has gone through you?"[15]

Heschel wrote about the Biblical prophets, the Talmudic
rabbis, the medieval philosophers, and the Hasidic saints of the
eighteenth and nineteenth centuries. He described prophecy in
the land of Israel, rabbinic scholarship in Babylonia (now Iraq),
philosophy in Spain and Egypt, and Jewish life in Eastern Europe. However, the common denominator amongst all these
journeys in time and space was Heschel's own quest for self-
understanding. He continually sought to perceive how the masters and sages of the past confronted the humanly universal and
particularly Jewish problems which vexed his own soul and
mind. Moses Maimonides, the twelfth century Jewish philosopher, was such a master.

In the course of describing Maimonides' inner life, Heschel
in effect predicted the turn his own life would take. In writing
Maimonides' biography, Heschel anticipated his own autobiog-
raphy. Unlike other scholars who understood Maimonides' life
and his philosophy as a paradigm of consistency, Heschel insisted that during the last ten years of his life, the focus of
Maimonides' interests radically shifted. Heschel claims that as
a result of a lifetime of "inner wrestling" and "self-questing," a
radical change was precipitated in Maimonides' life. Heschel
insists that Maimonides shifted his primary interest from scholarship to social action, from metaphysics to ethics, from
thoughts to deeds. A review of Heschel's life reveals a very
similar "dramatic change" during approximately the last ten
years of Heschel's life. In the 1960s and until his death in 1972,
Heschel was personally involved, on a major scale, with the
dominant social issues of those years. In addition, Heschel de-
voted time, thought, and action to the problems of youth,
aging, medical ethics, religious education, etc. But what may
have precipitated this change in the focus of Heschel's life?
What made him reverse his gaze from the past to the present,
from the realm of thought to the mine work of deeds? It may

be suggested that Heschel's personal encounter with the prophets of Israel, in the course of this quest for self-knowledge, led to this change of focus.

In the early 1960s, Heschel was preparing the English edition of his work on the prophets. It was this endeavor which precipitated the change. In a rare autobiographical statement, made in the course of a television interview taped a few days before his death, Heschel noted:

> May I make a personal statement here? I've written a book on the prophets, a rather large book. I spent many years. And, really, this book changed my life. Because early in my life, my great love was for learning, studying. And the place where I preferred to live was my study and books and writing and thinking. I've learned from the prophets that I have to be involved in the affairs of man, in the affairs of suffering man.[16]

For Abraham Heschel, the purpose of scholarship, of theological speculation is self-understanding. The thought must lead to the deed, the idea to the activity.

Religious Self-Understanding

Just as an individual is in a constant state of flux and development, so is a living religious tradition in perpetual motion. Just as an individual's life must be a constant exercise in self-understanding, so the life of a religious tradition must embrace a perpetual quest for self-understanding. Without persistent questing and questioning, a religious tradition is in danger of atrophy. The continuous process of self-examination is that which keeps a tradition alive and vibrant. It protects the religious mind from frigidity, the religious soul from fossilization. Thus, for Heschel, the specific task of religious philosophy is "religion's reflections upon its basic insights and basic attitudes, [the] *radical self-understanding of religion in terms of its own spirit.*"[17]

As a religious philosopher, specifically as a Jewish religious philosopher, Heschel felt obliged to dedicate himself to identifying the categories of thought by means of which religion in general, and Judaism in particular, may understand itself "in terms of its own spirit." Heschel warned against creating religion in our own likeness. Instead, he insisted upon understanding religion on its own terms.

Believing that "a religious way of thinking" exists, and that it is distinguishable from other ways of thinking, Heschel strove to depict the boundaries, the unique qualities, of religious thought. Heschel's first attempt in this monumental task was his doctoral dissertation, *Die Prophetie*. In this work, Heschel demonstrates how Biblical thinking radically differs from Greek thought, how the worldview of Western culture which was nurtured from ancient Greek thought is sharply distinct from Hebraic thinking which has its roots in the Hebrew Bible. Furthermore, Heschel maintains, the initiation and development of classical Western theology—Jewish, Christian, and Islamic—rest upon a basic misconception.

Since Philo of Alexandria, throughout the Middle Ages, and down to modern times, Heschel claims, an attempt has continually been made by theologians to demonstrate how Biblical thought is identical with current philosophical fashion. This endeavor, endemic to the classical theological enterprise, he asserts, rests upon a fundamental mistake. Biblical thought, he insists, is radically different from Greco-German philosophical thought. The Aristotelean God, for example, is "thought thinking itself"; the God of the prophets of Israel is a being characterized by his transitive concern about the human condition. The God of the philosophers expresses a self-reflexive concern; he is involved only with himself. The God of the prophets is emphatically involved in human affairs. The ideal personality for the philosophers, Heschel claims, is to be like God—sterile, static thought. The ideal personality for the Bible is to be like God—active, dynamic concern for the human condition. The task of the human being is to aspire for the prophetic gift.

Despite its massive intellectual contribution, classical theological speculation failed to understand Biblical thought. It
failed to perceive the unique categories of Biblical thinking and
imposed a foreign system of categories onto Biblical thought.
Thus, much of Western theology is the product of a hybrid of
ill-matched components. For Heschel, theology must not im-
pose external categories upon the sources of religious speculation, but must understand those sources in terms of their
intrinsic categories, in terms of their own spirit.

Not only Greco-German philosophy, but also more recently
articulated postulates of philosophy, psychology, and sociology
are inadequate tools for attaining religious self-understanding.
For Heschel, many of the "cultural assumptions" which most
contemporary people affirm are antithetical or irrelevant to Biblical thinking. To achieve religious self-understanding, the contemporary religious thinker must be aware of the nature and
implications of those cultural assumptions. He or she must take
caution before imposing them upon religious thinking, before
asserting their compatibility with religious thought.

For Heschel, religious thinking, rooted in the Hebrew Bible,
provides a perspective from which one can evaluate many of our
"cultural assumptions." Utilizing categories of Biblical thinking, Heschel polemicized against a number of notions popular
in modern thought.

Heschel berated attempts to confine religion to a sub-
category of philosophy, sociology, or psychology. He rejected
the efforts of those who reduce religion into something else,
who equate religion with something else, who define religion in
other than religious categories. For example, Heschel dis-
counted the endeavor to reduce and to equate religion in general and Judaism in particular, with rationalism. To do so, for
Heschel, meant to commit the "reductionist fallacy"; it represented "an intellectual evasion of the profound difficulties" of
faith, belief, and observance. For Heschel, rationalism cannot
provide an adequate standard for evaluating religious truth.
What is deemed reasonable in one age may be claimed unrea-

sonable in another age. Our perception of what is reasonable is too imprecise a tool with which to affirm an apprehension of truth.[18] Similarly, analytic philosophy and symbolic logic are incapable of examining claims to religious truth. In addition, they prove helpless in the face of personal and historical emergencies.

Though Heschel appreciated the use of scientific methods for resolving scientific problems, he dismissed the assertion that scientific methods are applicable to religious problems. For Heschel, "God is not a scientific problem, and scientific methods are not capable of solving it."[19] Though science may be capable of explaining phenomena which are part of reality and part of human existence, scientific method is an inadequate tool with which to examine all aspects of reality. He writes:

> There are aspects of given reality which are congruous with the categories of scientific logic, while there are aspects of reality which are inaccessible to this logic.[20]

A feature of scientific thinking and of Western philosophical tradition is the impetus to define everything, to compartmentalize experience. For Heschel, however, the central terms which epitomize religious thinking elude concise definitions. God cannot be defined, but only experienced. The "concept of God" is of penultimate importance; the presence of God is of ultimate significance. For Heschel, the religious quest begins not with definitions, but with an awareness of the ineffable. That which transcends comprehension, that which definitions cannot contain, is at the root of the religious consciousness.

To trap God, holiness, revelation, and prayer, in the artificial construct of imposed definitions would deprive them of their meaning, their power, their pertinence. Pivotal religious categories are neither rational nor irrational; rather, they are suprarational. Religious insight, religious self-understanding, emerges not from the realm of analysis, but from the realm of ineffability. Thus, for Heschel, concepts, definitions, and words are not "the last word"; rather, they are windows through which we may approach him who transcends both worlds and words.

As the categories of natural science are irrelevant to religious self-understanding, so are the categories of the social sciences. To reduce religious experience to sociological categories, for example, is to commit the "sociological fallacy." To reduce God to a symbol of the ideals of a social group, is to deflate him. To define prayer as being primarily an act of social identification is to distort the reality of prayer, to reduce the inner stirrings of the soul to a social amenity.

For Heschel there are more important questions for religious life than—to which sociological category may a religious group be assigned? For Heschel, the question of group affiliation must be eclipsed by the necessity for individual commitment. For Heschel, distinctions between right and wrong, sincerity and mendacity, authenticity and sham, are more important for spiritual existence than distinctions between people and religious groups.

According to Heschel, a sociological approach to moral and spiritual problems elevates social approval toward becoming a standard for determining good and evil, for discerning religious authenticity and religious apostasy. A sociological approach maintains that moral worth is primarily determined by how well one's deeds serve social ends. Human worth becomes determined by one's value to the group.

Heschel's experience in Nazi Germany convinced him that social approval and serving social ends cannot be viable standards for individual moral choice. Just as any individual may be wrong, so may a group be wrong. "A group may often act as accumulated selfishness, as the seat of demonic forces."[21] What is useful to the group may be wrong. Indeed, for Heschel, at times to conform to the group is to deform one's own soul. To evaluate the worth of an individual by how well he serves the group is to obscure the notion that the human being is intrinsically valuable. It is to deny the claim that a person's value derives from the fact that he is, and not from what he does. For Heschel, the primary question is not—what does the group demand?, but—what does God expect from me?

Heschel did not reject the sociological enterprise per se. He only cautioned against any attempt to reduce spiritual existence to sociological constructs and he indicated the potential moral implications of so doing. Similarly, Heschel did not oppose psychology per se; however, he did discount a tendency toward what he termed "panpsychology" which reduced spiritual and moral concerns to being the products of psychical processes and impulses.

In opposition to psychologists of religion who claimed that religion may be defined primarily as a quest for personal satisfaction, Heschel perceived the religious quest as an attempt to fulfill God's needs, God's desires. To those who maintain that religion is motivated by a desire for personal satisfaction, Heschel retorted that to the contrary—"religion is critique of satisfaction. Its end is joy, but its beginning is discontent, detesting boasts, smashing idols."[22]

In Heschel's view, the Freudians who maintain that religious beliefs are only attempts to satisfy subconscious wishes, that God is merely a projection of self-seeking emotions, fail to understand the authentic religious quest at all. To affirm God as "ego in disguise" is to forfeit authentic faith and to replace it with an idolatrous faith. To do so is to equate religious worship with self-worship. In an autobiographical aside, Heschel once remarked:

I had a very interesting experience recently during conversations with a distinguished psychologist. He said to me: "You know, the Freudian notion of human personality becomes totally irrelevant in our days. Who cares now whether he loved his aunt or didn't love his mother. This is not the issue! The real issue is—is there meaning in the world?"[23]

Though he does not mention Skinnerian psychology by name, Heschel often inveighs against the Skinnerian notion that adjustment to society is necessarily a goal toward which one must strive. For Heschel, adjustment to a society which "persists in squandering the material resources of the world on luxuries in a world where more than a billion people go to bed hungry every night," is not something towards which one should aspire.[24] To adjust to a society which furthers the inhuman use of human beings may be an indication of psychological "health," but it is also an indication of a sick soul. Heschel maintains that the religious endeavor fails in its quest for self-understanding when it proclaims adjustment as a necessary virtue. Religious self-understanding compels one to emulate Abraham, the father of Western religions. According to rabbinic tradition, Abraham's distinction was in *not* adjusting and conforming, but in defying and initiating. Judaism began with Abraham's destroying the idols of his father and of his society. For Heschel, therefore, religious self-understanding is primarily concerned not with resolving the Oedipus complex, but with instilling the "Abraham complex." According to Heschel, authentic "religion begins as a breaking off, as a going away. It continues in acts of nonconformity to idolatry."[25]

Because much of contemporary religious life and thought is not characterized by efforts at authentic religious self-understanding, because the "Abraham complex" is not nurtured by religious "establishments," religious life has become divorced from its authentic roots, according to Heschel. The decline of qualitative religious existence cannot be totally ascribed to influences of "secularization." For Heschel,

> it would be more honest to blame religion for its own defeats. Religion declined not because it was refuted, but because it became irrelevant, dull, oppressive, insipid. When faith is completely replaced by creed, worship by discipline, love by habit; when the crisis of today is ignored because of the splendor of the past; when faith becomes an heirloom rather than a living fountain; when religion speaks only in the name of authority rather than with the voice of compassion, its message becomes meaningless.[26]

According to Heschel, the current spiritual recession is because "we have bartered holiness for convenience, loyalty for success, love for power, wisdom for information, tradition for fashion."[27]

Thus, for Heschel, questing and questioning keep religion alive and vibrant. Mummifying the spirit, codifying past dogmas, can only insure an irrelevant, insipid, inauthentic faith. The quest for religious self-understanding is the pace-maker of the religious heart. In Heschel's portrayal of "depth theology," the notions of individual self-understanding and of religious self-understanding blend into one.

Depth Theology

For Abraham Heschel, the truth is that *the* truth cannot be known with any certainty. Heschel would have agreed with Franz Rosenzweig, the modern Jewish philosopher, who said, "Truth is a noun only for God; for man it is but an adjective." Since absolute truth eludes human comprehension, no religion, no philosophy, no ideology, can claim a monopoly on truth. For Heschel, therefore, the religious quest entails questions rather than conclusions. For the authentic religious thinker all conclusions are but a premise. Life is an ongoing battle for integrity, a never ending war against mendacity. The only weapon against self-deception is a commitment to persist in the search for self-understanding. Religious life is a pilgrimage rather than a panacea, a journey rather than a pollyanna. Only with death is the journey at an end. To believe we have arrived in the Promised Land while we are still in the wilderness is an act of self-delusion. He who believes he has found absolute truth is one who is truly lost. "He who thinks that he has finished *is* finished."[28]

For Heschel, therefore, "the central issue is not Truth in terms of a doctrine, but veracity, honesty, or sincerity in terms of personal existence."[29] For the individual, the quest for self-understanding, the struggle for integrity, honesty, and sincerity, takes precedence over impossible claims to absolute truth. For the religious thinker, for the religious personality, depth theology supersedes theological speculation and dogmatic concretization. Depth theology is for religious thought what self-reflection is for individual thought.

As the process of self-understanding emerges out of the totality of an individual's situation, depth theology expresses the totality of individual religious existence. Depth theology represents a fundamental attitude towards life and the world. Depth theology reflects the total religious consciousness and not just the workings of the mind. Depth theology is concerned with the pre-reflective, pre-theological, ineffable moment of inwardness in which God and man embrace. Depth theology expresses the act of faith, the private intimacy of the heart's stirrings and of the soul's yearnings. The insights of depth theology defy definitions and precede concise articulation.

Depth theology warns us against intellectual smugness. It provokes us to make our theological pronouncements consistent with our religious experiences. It compels us to insure that our concepts correlate with our commitments. It implants within us the impetus "to nurse the song in the recesses of the soul."[30]

At the heart of religious existence, depth theology is the necessary but not sufficient component of religious life and thought. Depth theology, the act of faith, must be balanced by theology, the content of belief. A polar balance must prevail: faith and belief, commitment and creed, event and idea, the spontaneity of religious experience and the regularity of religious ritual. Depth theology without theology is a soul without a body. Theology without depth theology is a body without a soul. Depth theology without theology is a blind, vagabond spirit. Without depth theology, theology becomes a paraplegic.

Theology speaks for the people; depth theology speaks for the individual. Theology strives for communication, for universality; depth theology strives for insight, for uniqueness.

Theology is like sculpture, depth theology is like music. Theology is in the books; depth theology is in the hearts. The former is doctrine, the latter is an event. Theologies divide us; depth theology unites us.[31]

Polarity

According to Heschel, the polarity which obtains between depth theology and theology, faith and creed, event and idea, is a key to understanding the dialectic which characterizes religious existence and religious self-understanding. Indeed, for Heschel, polarity is not only the key to religious self-understanding, but is a vehicle towards structuring our perception of reality.

In an essay entitled "Confusion of Good and Evil," which originally appeared in a volume of essays on the thought of his close friend Reinhold Niebuhr, Heschel expresses his pivotal notion of polarity: "To Jewish tradition, too, paradox is an essential way of understanding the world, history and nature. Strife, tension, contradiction characterize all of reality. . . . There is a polarity in everything except God. For all tension ends in God. He is beyond all dichotomies."[32]

Heschel understood the struggle for authentic religious existence to be characterized, for example, by a dynamic tension between doubt and belief, regularity and spontaneity, thought and deed. His writings reveal these tensions, and during his life Heschel struggled with the challenge they pose. Without such tension, Heschel maintained, theological atrophy would set in; facile solutions to complex problems would result.

In his careful study of the tenth-century Jewish philosopher Saadya Gaon, Heschel describes Saadya's inner life as a struggle to translate the act of faith into a creed, into the content of belief. While the medieval philosophies Saadya utilized to deal with his problem may not be relevant to us today, the record of his personal quest is pertinent, Heschel maintains. For Saadya's quest is our quest: how to translate the insights of the act of faith into a statement of beliefs; how to utilize doubt as a vehicle to a firmer faith. Indeed, Heschel himself spent much of his time attempting to do just that.

Heschel's *God in Search of Man* must be seen as the polar opposite of his work on prayer and religious symbolism, *Man's Quest for God*. For Heschel, the religious experience is a tension between God's initiative and the human response to that initiative, between the revelation of God to human beings in the Bible and in historical events and man's response in prayer, study, and interpretation of the sacred texts which record revelatory events.

Heschel wrote profusely, in three languages, about a variety of Hasidic masters. Here, too, a polar tension is evident between two varieties of Hasidic masters. This polarity is most clearly evident in Heschel's last book, *A Passion for Truth*, in which he discusses the founder of Hasidism, the Baal Shem Tov, and the great dissenter of Hasidism, Rabbi Mendel of Kotsk. These two personalities represented a struggle between love and justice, mercy and truth, community and individualism, pleasure and asceticism, the quest for exaltation, and the harsh task of self-scrutiny. In an autobiographical preface to this work, written shortly before his death, Heschel noted that the tension he identified between these two Hasidic masters was a tension which he had incorporated into his own life.

In his two-volume Hebrew *magnum opus* on rabbinic theology, Heschel identified two trends in Jewish thought which characterize its history and development. Heschel effectively argued that Judaism is not a monolithic faith but the product of a dynamic tension between the mystical and the rational. His painstaking, erudite analysis of this tension echoes a tension in his own soul between the mystic and the rationalist, the poet and the philosopher. Thus, for Heschel, the notion of polarity, the dialectic between polar opposites, provides a vehicle toward self-understanding and toward religious self-analysis. For Heschel, the polarity at the root of human reality and of religious existence is the polarity of the infinite God and finite man. Man without God is a conclusion without a premise. God without mankind is a king without a kingdom. Man without God is a creature without a creator. Without man, there is no being to embody the image of God. In the discussion which follows, we shall first offer a summary of Heschel's views of God, of man, and finally, of the relationships between the two.

God

Heschel's theology is not anthropocentric, but theocentric. All paths to knowledge, all roads to discernment must lead towards God. The purpose of the human quest for self-understanding, too, must be to place God at the center of our lives and of our thoughts. What Karl Marx said about Ludwig Feuerbach's treatment of Hegel may be said of Heschel's treatment of much of classical and contemporary theology, "He stood them on their heads." For Heschel, religion is not to be primarily perceived as the fulfillment of a psychological need of man, but as a need of God. The Bible is to be read more as God's anthropology than as man's theology—what God has to say about and to us, rather than what we think about him. Not man's search for God, but God's search for man, and the human response to that quest, ought to be identified as the primary religious concern. Thus, Heschel's philosophy of religion is a Copernican revolution. Copernicus saw the sun—not the earth—as the center of the universe. Heschel sees God rather than man at the core of the theological enterprise. By putting God at the center of human existence, Heschel adopts the opposite position of that held by his fellow Jewish existentialist, Martin Buber. For Buber, man is at the center. The human "I" seeks out the Eternal "Thou," God. For Heschel, God is "I" and the "Thou" is man. God is subject, the focal point of existence.

Karl Marx in criticizing Hegel's *Philosophy of Right* wrote, "To be *radical* is to grasp the root of the matter. But for man the root is man himself." Not so for Heschel. For him, God, the "Root of Roots," is the root.

Following the Hebrew Bible and the Jewish mystics, Heschel rejected the assumption that human beings may know the essence of God. God may be apprehended, but not comprehended. We may not know God's nature; we may only apprehend and experience God as he is manifest to us in history, in nature and in sacred books. We do not know *what* God is. We only know *how* God is when he encounters us and when we respond to his gestures. In Heschel's words:

> The Bible tells us nothing about God in Himself; all its sayings refer to His relations to man. His own life and essence are neither told nor disclosed. . . . The only events in the life of God the Bible knows are acts done for the sake of man: acts of creation, acts of redemption, or acts of revelation.[33]

By means of revelation, God invites us to become part of a chapter in his biography, to play a role in a scene of the cosmic drama with him. In so doing, we apprehend God only as he is manifest in one chapter of his eternal life, in a short single scene contained in the drama of time and timelessness, in an instantaneous heart-beat of the pulse of creation. What he really is, how he appears in other chapters, in other scenes, in other worlds, is beyond the ken of our knowledge. We are invited to enter the inner life of God, but only as it is manifest to us in creation and in human experience. As a child experiences his or her father in the relationship of father to child, but does not understand the essence of his or her father, so we experience God's inner life only in his relationship to us, but not in his essence. Thus, for Heschel, the essence of God eludes us, but the presence of God in the world and in history must concern us. Here, too, Heschel follows the approach of the Jewish mystics. Like these mystics, Heschel maintains that God in essence transcends human apprehension and comprehension. However, God as he manifests himself in our world, our history, our lives, invites us to open our hearts to him, to have our inner lives cleave to his inner life. In this regard, in an essay on "The Mystical Element in Judaism," Heschel wrote:

> This is the pattern of Jewish mysticism: to have an open heart for the inner life of God. It is based on two assumptions: that there is an inner life in God and that the existence of man ought to revolve in a spiritual dynamic course around the life of God.[34]

Man

For Heschel, defining the nature of the human being is not an objective, speculative, or clinical task. In describing man, we are describing ourselves. In defining man, we are defining ourselves. We are the subject of our own inquiry. We are a subject seeking our own predicate. Thus, the quest for human understanding is an exercise in self-definition, in self-understanding. As Heschel put it, "In establishing a definition of man I am defining myself. Its first test must be acceptability to myself."[35]

In the course of developing his own view of the nature of man, Heschel has occasion to analyze and to discuss definitions of man, classical and modern. The first group of definitions Heschel considers are those which define man as a kind of animal.

Aristotle had defined man as a variety of animal. For Aristotle, man is a "political animal," a "civilized animal," an "imitative animal." Scholastic philosophy had accepted Aristotle's other definition of man as a "rational animal." Benjamin Franklin defined man as a "tool making animal."

While Heschel does not reject the zoological validity of classifying man as a variety of animal, he does insist that zoologically oriented definitions of man are too limited, too incomplete. Though man may be an animal, he is more than an animal. To define man only as an animal is to dehumanize man, to deflate human dignity. The moral implication of defining man as an animal is that if man is only an animal, he may justifiably be treated as an animal. For Heschel, the nature of man may be determined by emphasizing man's contrasts rather than his similarities with animals. For one to accept a definition of man which depicts man as a kind of animal, one has to think of oneself as a kind of animal. Before assenting to such a definition one must ask oneself: "Do I recognize myself in any of these definitions? Am I ready to identify myself as an animal with a particular adjective?" For Heschel, "man in search of self-understanding is not motivated by a desire to classify himself zoologically or to find his place in the animal kingdom." Man is in search of his humanity and not his animality. "He is not in search of his origin, he is in search of his destiny." Thus, for Heschel, defining man in animal terms is not an exercise in self-understanding but an expression of self-insult.[36]

As Heschel rejects the tendency to understand man as an animal, so he disclaims the more modern trend to define man as a kind of machine. This approach depicts man as "an ingenious array of portable plumbing," "a machine into which we put what we call food and produce what we call thought." Even in slang we speak of ourselves as being "turned on," "turned off," "geared up," as having "our motors running." For Heschel, this definition of man is also inadequate. Human existence is a mystery, a marvel. A machine is an invention, an artificial construct.

To define man as a machine implies dangerous moral implications. A human being is irreplaceable, but once he is thought of as a machine he becomes replaceable. A machine is cared for as long as it is useful and productive. To define man as a machine would mean that once one is no longer useful and productive, one can be dispensed with. If man is an animal, his physician becomes a veterinarian, and if man is a machine, his physician becomes a mechanic. For Heschel, man is created in the image of God, and not in the image of an automobile.

An often quoted definition of man reduces the human body

to its chemical equivalents. "'The human body contains a sufficient amount of fat to make seven cakes of soap, enough iron to make a medium sized nail . . . ,'" etc. Reflecting upon this proposed definition, Heschel suggests, "Perhaps there was a connection between this statement and what the Nazis actually did in the extermination camps: make soap out of human flesh."[37]

For Heschel, the aforementioned definitions of man are conceptually inadequate and morally dangerous. They are oversimplifications. When applied to actual human beings they prove barren.[38]

To achieve a more complete, more acceptable understanding of the nature of man, Heschel recommends describing man rather than defining him. Definitions of man confine more than they portray. They conceal more than they reveal. They stifle more than they convey. To define man only from a single perspective is to eclipse other dimensions of human nature, other characteristics of the human being, other manifestations of being human. To confine man to a definitional straitjacket is to paint a portrait with half a face, to portray a moon in a state of eclipse. In order to convey a more complete picture, more than one pole of human existence must be provided. Consequently, in his description of man, Heschel again adopts a polar approach. Man may be described in terms of a polarity. Human existence embraces a polarity of human being and being human; creation from dust and creation in the divine image; sameness and uniqueness; finiteness and eternity; solitude and solidarity.

Heschel extracts this polar understanding of human nature from the Hebrew Bible. In the Hebrew Bible man is described both as a creature created in the image of God (Gen. 1:26) and as "dust and ashes" (Gen. 18:27; Job 42:6). In Heschel's words, "Man, then, is involved in a polarity of a divine image and worthless dust."[39]

To understand the meaning of the Biblical view of the nature of man, one must penetrate the meaning of the allusive term "image of God." What does it mean to say that man is created in the Divine image? Heschel offers a number of possible interpretations.

Since God is invisible, no one could see him. Since God is invisible, his presence in the world might not be perceived. God, therefore, created a reminder, an image—man. Man is a reminder of God. One looks at man and is reminded of the presence of God and of our obligations to him.

The Bible describes no creature other than man as having been created in the image of God. That man is so described indicates that he is essentially different from other creatures. As the image of God, human existence has intrinsic worth, inherent dignity. Human worth derives not from our deeds, our achievements, our talents, but from having been created in the image of the Creator.

As a reminder of God, as the image of God, man is obliged to emulate God. This means that as God is compassionate, man must be compassionate. As God strives for meaning and justice, man is obliged to seek meaning beyond absurdity and to do justice. As God loves mankind, man must love his neighbor as himself. As God is holy, man must strive for holiness; he must aspire for sanctity. Man created in the image of God refers not to an analogy of *being*, but to an analogy of *doing*.

As God, the Creator, is unique, man, his creature is unique. According to rabbinic thought, man's creation in the image of God signifies not only human creaturehood, but human creativity. Man is created with the ability to create. Man is God's partner in completing, in perfecting "the work of creation." While "the Greek thinkers sought to understand man as part of the universe; the prophets sought to understand man as a partner of God."[40]

Man's partnership with God, man's covenant with God, demonstrates how seriously God takes man, how deeply God is committed to mankind, how involved a partisan God is regarding the human struggle for meaning and for love. This exaltation of humankind, however, is not an invitation to indolence, not an entree to human conceit, but a challenge to human responsiveness, a proclamation of human responsibility. Only fulfillment of God's expectation can justify man's exaltation.

The divine gift of human freedom invests mankind not only with power but with responsibility. By freely entering into a partnership with God, man thereby becomes responsible for the destiny of God's dreams and designs. Man becomes co-responsible for the fate of God's world and for the fate of God's presence in the world. Human existence is co-existence with God.

"Man is man not because of what he has in common with the earth, but because of what he has in common with God."[41] The link between God and man is the covenant between God and man. The covenant embodies God's commitment to man and his expectations of man. The covenant means that God is profoundly involved in human history. The covenant signifies that man without God is a conclusion without a premise, that God without man is a king without a kingdom. Man without God is a non-sequitur, a fallacy. The covenant is the knot which binds God to man, the premise to the conclusion, the abscissa to the ordinate, the king to his kingdom, the human need for meaning to the divine need for human righteousness. The covenant is a product of God's revelation to man and of man's response to the revelatory event. To further penetrate Heschel's view of the relationship between God and man, we must consider his understanding of revelation.

Revelation

Heschel chose to invest most of his scholarly efforts laboring to unravel the mystery of the divine-human encounter in history known as "revelation." The central concern of Heschel's books, *The Prophets, God in Search of Man, The Theology of Ancient Judaism* (Hebrew), and of his major Hebrew essays, "Prophecy in the Middle Ages," "Did Maimonides Aspire for Prophetic

Inspiration?", is the phenomenon of revelation. For Heschel, religion begins with revelation. Therefore, to understand the nature of religion, to attain religious self-understanding, one must attempt to penetrate the meaning and the mystery of the revelatory experience.

According to Heschel, revelation is unique; it is the essential, basic event of religious life. To discuss revelation, therefore, categories and criteria which fall outside of the boundaries of religious self-understanding pall into irrelevancy.

The natural and social sciences have natural and social phenomena as the objects of their investigations. Supernaturalistic phenomena such as revelation fall outside their purview. A supra-rationalistic event, revelation cannot be competently analyzed by rationalistic philosophy. "Revelation is a mystery for which reason has no concepts."[42] A meta-historical event, revelation cannot be relegated to historical categories. Thus, only through religious self-understanding, and not through utilization of the tools of other ways of thinking, may we begin to try to fathom the mystery of the revelatory event and the pressing pertinence of its implications.

The nature of revelation, Heschel maintains, is locked up in the realm of the ineffable. The essence of the revelatory event is inscrutable. Just as the people of Israel stood at the fringes of Sinai, so do we stand at the borders when trying to penetrate the mystery of revelation.

While the Bible introduces us to the mystery of revelation, it does not seek to penetrate or to fully explain it. Rather than providing a description of revelation, the Bible provides a report of man's experience of revelation. And man's experience of revelation is but a part of what happened in revelation. Therefore, we cannot equate the event of revelation with man's experience of revelation. Nor may we identify a report of man's experience of revelation with the event of revelation itself. Nevertheless, that report—the words of the Biblical narrative—is all we have. "All we can do is to try to sense the unworded across its words."[43] Though the essence of revelation eludes us, we may strive to comprehend the message of the Biblical report of man's encounter with God. We may attempt to perceive what happened to those to whom God directly revealed his word and his will, i.e., to the prophets of Israel.

In his work, *The Prophets*, Heschel penetrates the inner lives of the prophets in order to ascertain how the prophets perceived their encounters with God. Heschel's analysis of the prophetic consciousness is an attempt to understand what it meant to think, feel, respond, and act like a prophet.

Heschel's description of the prophetic consciousness primarily emerges from a careful study of the books of the literary prophets of the Hebrew Bible such as Amos, Hosea, Jeremiah, and Isaiah. From this intensive investigation, Heschel concludes that the prophets offered no "concept" of God, no exposition regarding the nature of God. Instead, they provided an exposition of God's insight into man and his concern for man. "They disclosed attitudes *of* God rather than ideas *about* God."[44] Though they did not reveal the essence of God, the prophets did reveal the perspective of God. Having pierced the inner life of God, the prophets saw the world through the eyes of God. Thus, the prophets and the Bible provide God's anthropology rather than man's theology—God's thoughts about man rather than man's understanding of God.

What do the prophets see through the eyes of God about man and his relationship to God? How does the reflection of man appear in God's eyes when he gazes upon his creation?

For the prophets, as for the entire Hebrew Bible, human history consists of individual episodes in one great drama: the quest of God for man and man's flight from God. For the prophet, God's life with man is characterized by God's expectations and man's persistent frustration of those expectations. Human experience embraces a dialectic of God's dreams and history's nightmares.

Rather than reveal the divine essence, the prophets proclaimed the divine will, the divine word. While mysticism indicates the human quest for God, prophecy pronounced the divine quest for man, the divine concern for the human situation.

While the gods of mythology are portrayed as being egotistical and the God of Aristotle is described as the a-pathetic unmoved mover, the God of the prophets is the "most moved mover." The prophets revealed that God is a God of pathos, profoundly concerned and involved with man. The prophet is a person who sympathizes with the divine pathos. He shares God's concern for the pathetic condition of his creation and of his world.

The prophets observed that revelation, like history, is not a monologue of God, but a dialogue of God and man, of God with man. Revelation, therefore, is a co-revelation, of God to man and of man to God. Revelation embraces both God's turning to man and man's turning towards God. There must be a "receiving of the Torah" as well as a "giving of the Torah." When the people fail to respond to the divine initiative, the prophet shares dismay with God.

The Human Response: Faith

"There is only one way to define Jewish religion," according to Heschel.

> It is the awareness of God's interest in man, the awareness of a covenant, of a responsibility that lies on Him as well as on us. Our task is to concur with His interest, to carry out His vision of our task. God is in need of man for the attainment of His ends, and religion, as Jewish tradition understands it, is a way of serving these ends, of which we are in need, even though we may not be aware of them, ends which we must learn to feel the need of.[45]

God's need of man is a self-imposed concern. It is our task to fulfill that need.

The nature of God's need of man, God's ends which we are obliged to serve, the stipulations to which we are bound in our contract with God, are contained in the Bible, the record of revelation and in the ongoing interpretation of the Bible by religious tradition. Basically, what God requires is our righteousness, our faithfulness, our commitment, our sacred deeds.

For Heschel, "religion begins with the certainty that something is asked of us, that there are ends which are in need of us."[46] While others have defined religion as a feeling of human dependence upon God, Heschel maintains that religious life means that God depends upon us, upon our deeds.

In opposition to Paul Tillich who taught that God is the "ground of being," Heschel taught that "God is above the ground," that God is a source of qualms, of demands. God, as understood by Tillich, requires nothing of us. God, as understood by Heschel, has needs which may be satisfied by our deeds.[47] While Paul Tillich spoke of God as man's ultimate concern, Heschel speaks of man as God's ultimate concern. For Heschel, religion requires both a "leap of action" as well as "a leap of faith."

According to the philosopher Descartes, "I think; therefore, I am." According to the Bible, as interpreted by Heschel, "I am commanded—therefore I am."[48] According to the German philosopher, Immanuel Kant, "I ought, therefore I can." According to the Bible, "Thou art commanded, therefore, thou canst."[49]

Though God is in search of man, man is not always responsive to the divine initiative. In Heschel's words, "there is an eternal cry in the world: God is beseeching man. Some are startled; others remain deaf. We are all looked for. An air of expectancy hovers over life. Something is asked of man, of all men."[50]

Rather than respond to God, man often hides from God. When Adam and Eve hid from his presence, God called: "Where are you?" (Gen. 3:9) In each generation, when man hides from God, the call goes out again: where are you? This question is the quest of God in search of man. The answer is faith in God. Religious existence includes God's question and man's answer, God's initiative and man's response, God in search of man and man's quest for God.

Faith is our response to God's overwhelming presence, to God's challenge to us, to God's demands of us. Faith is the polar opposite of creed. Faith is the act of believing; creed is the content of belief. For Heschel, "faith" is a transitive-active verb; "creed" is an abstract noun.

Faith is part of the human quest for the meaning beyond absurdity, for the meaning beyond mystery. Faith is an answer to God's question, and a challenge to all answers. As Heschel puts it:

> Well-adjusted people think that faith is an answer to all human problems. In truth, however, faith is a challenge to all human answers. Faith is a consuming fire, consuming all pretensions. To have faith is to be in labor.[51]

Faith puts God at the center of our lives. The truly faithful person, Heschel claims, will *not* say "I believe in God." To do so is to put our "I" before God. For the truly faithful person, "because God exists, I am able to believe."[52] Thus, faith begins with God. Our ability to believe in God is a gift from God.

For Heschel, faith is a bequest from God that must be won. Faith must be wrested from a human condition saturated with adversity. To have faith is to be able to believe in God in spite of God. To assert faith means to be optimists against our better judgment.

Faith is not a *creatio ex nihilo*. "There is no faith at first sight." The attainment of true faith is the result of an ongoing battle with absurdity rather than the product of an unconditional surrender to sterile creeds. For the faithful person, it is better to be defeated with God than to be victorious without God. Thus, for Heschel, faith entails risk rather than resignation, leaps of commitment rather than lip-service to hollow creeds. Faith is not the quest for illumination, but the struggle to perceive a glimmer of God's presence within the dark alleys of history. Faith is the polar opposite of revelation. In revelation God reveals his presence to the world. Through faith, we reveal God's presence to the world. In revelation God reveals his presence to us. Through faith we reveal our presence to him.

For Heschel, faith is not a part-time job, but a total commitment. Faith is not a hobby, but a life-style. From the perspective of faith, "God is of no importance unless He is of supreme importance."[53]

A response of the total person, faith is more than mere intellectual assent. More than assent to an idea, faith is consent to God. This is not to claim, however, that faith is immune to reason. For Heschel, "reason is a necessary co-efficient of faith. . . . Faith without reason is mute; reason without faith is blind."[54] In itself, faith is supra-rational. But without the polar balance provided by reason, faith is in danger of becoming a phantom of the imagination. Though faith is a weapon against absurdity, faith should not demand an assent to that which is intellectually absurd. Tertullian's motto—*Credo quia absurdum est* (I believe it because it is absurd)—is alien to the Jewish notion of faith.

According to Heschel, individual faith is necessary but not sufficient. Without an attachment to the treasurehouse of one's tradition, individual faith becomes a potential orphan. A single soul is too feeble to erect a sturdy bridge that leads to God. While each individual must plot his or her own route towards God, each individual is obliged to recognize that the roads traveled have been blazed and paved by those who came before us. The signposts along the way were erected long ago. Without the efforts of the past, without the experiences of the spiritual pioneers of religious tradition, our journey toward God might culminate in a circuitous route to nowhere, or, in a dead end. For Heschel, therefore, individual faith means making a new start down an old road.

In the quest for spiritual wealth, there are no Horatio Algers. In the struggle for faith, there are no self-made men. Only deposits made by our ancestors can adequately support us. Only the inexhaustible cumulative experiences of our tradition can sustain us. An individual soul cannot generate enough faith to sustain itself. A self-made man is prone to worship his creator, rather than to worship the Creator.

Jewish faith, according to Heschel, assumes recollection of that which happened to the people of Israel in past generations. Faith is not primarily an assent to great ideas, but a memory of great events. Rather than requiring intellectual affirmations of abstract ideas, Biblical faith emphasizes memory of concrete events. The redemption from Egypt, a historical experience, dominates Biblical and subsequent Jewish thought. Experience is the foundation for religious ideas. Theological concepts are penultimate to memories of divine acts. Our expectation for future redemption is grounded in our ancestors' experiences of past redemptions. Our belief in the revelation at Sinai is not merely an article of creed, but an experience of our forebears. Our belief is a shared memory of their experiences. By means of attachment to those memories, their experiences vicariously become our experiences. On Passover, for example, when each Jew recalls the Exodus from Egypt, each Jew thereby becomes a participant in the redemption from Egypt. The liturgy for the Passover meal, the *Seder*, reminds each Jew that "in every generation each Jew should regard himself as though he personally went forth from Egypt. . . . It was not only our forefathers whom the Holy One, praised be He, redeemed from slavery, but us also did He redeem together with them."

Faith, for Heschel, involves a polarity between present and past, individual and community, personal quests and ancient experiences. Religious faith entails being a pioneer as well as an heir, loyalty to historical events and faithfulness to individual experiences. To be authentic, faith must be rooted in tradition; however, to be vital faith must be more than an echo of tradition. Without the experiences of our ancestors, our faith is spiritually impoverished. Without our continual reaffirmation of faith, the faith of our fathers becomes a lost, buried treasure. Without memories of the experiences of our ancestors, our faith is destined to collapse like a skyscraper without a foundation.

Without our providing the link between their history and our destiny, the faith of our fathers may be fossilized forever.

The Human Response: Deeds

There is no instrument with which faith can be measured. Faith cannot be quantified, but it can be expressed; it can be verified. Our deeds express our beliefs; they verify the sincerity of our commitments.

There are no conclusive proofs for the existence of God, Father and Creator of all. There are only witnesses. By means of faith we bear witness to God's existence and to his presence in the world. Our deeds validate our faith in him. Our acts bear witness to him. If our deeds contradict our beliefs, we transgress a pivotal commandment; we "bear false witness." In this regard, Heschel was fond of quoting the bold statement of the ancient rabbis, "You are my witnesses (says God) and I am God (Isaiah 43:12, 13). Says Rabbi Shimon bar Yohai—(This verse means) if you are my witnesses, I am God; if you are not my witnesses, it is as if I am not God." Thus, in Heschel's thought, a polarity exists between faith and creed, between faith and deed. By performance of sacred deeds we concretize our faith in God; we justify God's faith in us.

"Faith is but a seed, while the deed is its growth or decay."[55] Unless our "leap of faith" leads to a "leap of action," our beliefs will be stillborn. Our deeds can give life to our affirmations of faith. Our deeds objectify our faith. They give form to our beliefs. They provide our convictions with a body as well as with a soul. "We realize that to *perform* is to lend *form* to a divine theme; that our task is to set forth the divine in acts, to express the spirit in tangible forms."[56]

The human being is a composite of soul, mind, and body, representing the spiritual, intellectual, and physical dimensions of human existence. Faith is a song the soul sings to God. Creed is an aria of ideas our minds dedicate to God. The sacred deed, the *mitzvah*, is the instrument upon which our body offers its symphony to God. Living in a physical world, man requires a physical means of worshiping God. "If man were only mind, worship in thought would be the form in which to commune with God. But man is body and soul, and his goal is so to live that both 'his heart and his flesh should sing to the living God.' "[57]

By means of a physical act of love, we can strengthen our feelings of love. In making love, we may strengthen our commitment to our beloved. Similarly, through the performance of sacred deeds we may strengthen faith, fortify belief, intensify commitment. According to Heschel, in doing more than we understand, we come to understand more than we do. "What cannot be grasped in reflection, we comprehend in deeds."[58]

For Heschel, the Pauline doctrine of justification by faith alone, cannot be justified. In Heschel's words, "Judaism stands and falls with the idea of the absolute relevance of human deeds. Even to God we ascribe the deed. *Imitatio dei* is in deeds. The deed is the source of holiness."[59] Thus, the performance of sacred deeds is our way of articulating our having been created in the image of God. By means of a physical act we can establish our link to, our likeness of the Divine. In a physical deed we may join the physical and the spiritual. In doing that which is finite, we may perceive that which is infinite. "In a sacred deed, we echo God's suppressed chant; in loving we intone God's unfinished song. No image of the Supreme may be fashioned, save one: our own life as an image of His will."[60]

Each *mitzvah*, each sacred deed, is one detail of the covenant with God. The *mitzvah*, the sacred deed, is the means to fulfilling our covenant with God. Heschel asks and answers: "What is a sacred deed? An encounter with the divine; a way of living in fellowship with God; a flash of holiness in the darkness of profanity . . . . "[61]

In the course of discussing religious observance, Heschel has occasion once again to make distinctions between Biblical thinking and Greco-German philosophical thought. Greek thought ponders the question of ontology: what is being? Biblical thought ponders: what is doing? Greek thought seeks to define human *being*. Biblical thought compels us to perform acts which express our being human. "Greek philosophy is concerned with *values*; Jewish thought dwells on *mitsvot*."[62] Values derive from man; *mitsvot* derive from God. Greek moral philosophy is primarily concerned with the good. Biblical thought is obsessed with the holy. The philosopher, Immanuel Kant, proposed that the basic question in ethics is—what I ought to do. The Biblical approach proposes that the basic question in ethics is meta-ethical—what does God require me to do?

For Heschel, a system of ethics based upon human rationality or social utility is too precarious, too unreliable. Any act may be justified in the name of social utility; any deed may be rationalized away as being morally proper. Neither is the conscience an infallible source for moral behavior. The conscience is but one voice amongst many within ourselves.

> The power of selfishness may easily subdue the pangs of conscience. . . . The conscience is not a legislative power, capable of teaching us what we ought to do but rather a preventive agency; a brake, not a guide; a fence, not a way. It raises its voice after a wrong deed has been committed, but often fails to give us direction in advance of our actions.[63]

Thus, for Heschel, the source of moral behavior cannot be derived from a human source alone. Only an exegesis of the divine will can provide an adequate foundation for human deeds, for sacred acts.

According to Heschel, the performance of sacred deeds does not secure human redemption. It only helps insure human integrity. Sacred deeds may not redeem us, but they make us worthy of being redeemed. Nevertheless, sacred deeds may retard the spread of evil; they may accelerate the initiation of redemption. They are incapable, however, of vanquishing evil; they are incapable of guaranteeing redemption: "At the end of days, evil will be conquered by the One; in historical times, evils must be conquered one by one."[64] Man's task, therefore, is not to redeem the world, but to make preparations for the final redemption. Sacred deeds are spiritual opportunities, adventures of the soul. Each act has the power either to advance or to obstruct the drama of redemption.

The Human Response: Prayer

"What is a *mitzvah*, a sacred act? *A Prayer in the form of a deed.*"[65] In order to understand Heschel's views on sacred deeds, one must survey his view of prayer. In order to fully comprehend Heschel's view of prayer, one must be aware of his view of sacred deeds.

For Heschel, prayer is the touchstone of all sacred deeds, the queen of all the commandments. "Each of our acts must be carried out as variations on the theme of prayer."[66] Our deeds either verify or refute the commitments we express during prayer. Our deeds can either desecrate or exalt the content of our prayers.

We are what we pray. "Prayer is to the soul what nourishment is to the body."[67] Without prayer, the soul starves and withers. The ability to pray is what makes us truly human. Man may be defined as the only creature who prays. "He who has never prayed is not fully human."[68]

An expression of being human, prayer is also a response to God's call. "Prayer is an answer to God: 'Here am I.' "[69] Prayer bridges the gap between man and God. Prayer prevents the gap from becoming an abyss. Prayer is the companionship of God and our soul. "To pray is to dream in league with God, to envision His holy visions."[70]

Prayer is to religion what thinking is to philosophy. Yet, prayer is not thinking. "To the thinker, God is an object; to the man who prays, He is the subject."[71] In prayer, the self is not the hub, but the spoke of a revolving wheel. In prayer, God becomes the center, the hub of our existence. The purpose of prayer is not to know him, but to be known to him, to be a thought in the mind of God. Prayer may begin as an exercise in self-understanding. However, to be authentic, prayer must conclude in the discovery of the self in relation to God.

By inviting God to enter our lives, to intervene in our affairs, we discover our self in relation to God. Moving from self-interest to self-surrender, our minds are liberated from the narrowness of self-interest. We behold our situation from the perspective of God, we take counsel with what we know about the will of God. We become able to discern between the significant and the trivial elements of our existence. We discover our true aspirations, the pangs we ignore, the longings we have forgotten. For Heschel, the primary purpose of prayer is not to make requests of God, but to discern God's demands upon us.

Man is a messenger of God who has forgotten the message. Through prayer, our amnesia is cured. We reaffirm our vocation as God's messenger, as God's agent. His needs become our deeds; his hopes become our aspirations; his dreams become our challenge. We realize that every person is charged with being God's vicar on earth. Prayer is not a replacement for deeds, but rather a catalyst for deeds. Prayer must be an inspiration for our acts of dedication.

3

Significance

ABRAHAM HESCHEL was a religious therapist treating the spiritual breakdown of our times. He taught us that life must be a perpetual quest for self-understanding, a perennial struggle with absurdity, a continual battle for meaning and integrity. He compels each of us to realize that to be what we are, we must become more than we are. He provokes each of us to apprehend life as an exercise in self-transcendence. He cajoles each of us to work on the great work of art called our own existence. He pleads for life to be a song, for human existence to be a celebration. For Heschel, life is a question to which each of us can become an answer.

According to Heschel, human existence is co-existence with God; to exist is to assist God. The categorical imperative of religious existence is to adjust our understanding to God rather than to adjust God to our understanding, to make the world relevant to God's vision rather than to make faith relevant to our whims and desires. To begin to satisfy this imperative, religious self-understanding is required.

For Jews and Christians, religious self-understanding begins with a commitment to the Hebrew Bible as Holy Scripture. Heschel reminded us that while we have much to say about the Bible, the Bible has much more to say about us. Heschel demonstrated the intellectual and existential relevance of Biblical thinking to contemporary human existence.

Nazi Germany was one of many indications that the cultural securities of much of Western civilization are unreliable, according to Heschel. Since the premises of Western civilization have "not withstood the stream of cruelty and crime that burst forth out of the undercurrents of evil in the human soul,"[72] perhaps one should look elsewhere for guidance and for meaning. Perhaps one should realize that Biblical thinking provides a viable alternative for dealing with the problems which vex us, the perplexities which confront us, the absurdities which dismay us. Heschel's life and thought, words and deeds, are evidence that "the Bible is not behind the times; it is ages ahead of our aspirations."[73] For Heschel, "the future of the western world will depend upon the way in which we relate ourselves to the Hebrew Bible."[74]

Significance for Christians

By showing how alive, how compelling, how pertinent, are the teachings of the prophets of Israel, Heschel made Christians aware of how alive and vital are the faith of Israel and the people of Israel. He reminded Christians "that a world without [the people of] Israel will be a world without the God of Israel."[75] He noted that "the marvel of Jewish existence, the survival of holiness in the history of the Jews, is a continuous verification of the marvel of the Bible. Revelation to Israel continues as revelation through Israel." Heschel recounts that when "the Protestant pastor, Christian Furchtegott Gellert, was asked by Frederick the Great, 'Herr Professor, give me proof of the Bible, but briefly, for I have little time,' Gellert answered, 'Your Majesty, the Jews.'"[76]

In 1963, *Christian Century* magazine invited Heschel to express his views on "Protestant renewal."[77] In so doing, Heschel offered the respectful suggestion that authentic Protestant self-renewal should be linked to a Protestant self-discovery of its roots in Judaism in general, and in the Hebrew Bible in particular. Heschel maintained that the process of the dejudaization of Christianity and the desanctification of the Hebrew Bible only pave the way for the abandonment of Christian origins and the alienation of Christianity from the core of its message.

In Heschel's view, the initial message of Christianity was corrupted by Christian theology's emphasis upon Hellenistic thought in place of Biblical thought. Only a conscious commitment to the roots of Christianity in Judaism, Heschel maintained, can save Christianity from self-distortion, from inauthenticity.

As a Jewish ambassador to the Christian world, Heschel vigorously campaigned against the notion of "mission to the Jews," against Christian efforts to convert Jews to Christianity. With typical frankness Heschel insisted that Christianity, as a daughter religion of Judaism, is required by the Ten Commandments to revere its parent religion. Respect rather than contempt, appreciation rather than repudiation, co-existence rather than supersession, ought to dominate Christian thinking about Jews and Judaism. Heschel claimed that Christians who continue to maintain the doctrine of "mission to the Jews," who view Jews only as potential Christians, suffer from "a spiritual Oedipus complex."

Amongst American Protestant theologians, Heschel's close friend Reinhold Niebuhr, was the first to denounce the validity of Christian efforts at proselytization of Jews. In the Catholic community, however, it took Heschel's persistent efforts in dialogues with popes John XXIII and Paul VI, to convince the Catholic Church to renounce the notion of "mission to the Jews." The Ecumenical Council's "Schema on the Jews" reveals the products of Heschel's efforts.

For Heschel, Jewish-Christian dialogue is predicated upon three assumptions: the absence of the charge of "deicide" against Jews, the absence of the notion of "mission to the Jews," and, the presence of faith—"the first and most important *prerequisite of interfaith is faith*."[78]

What binds Judaism and Christianity together, what necessitates inter-religious dialogue, is the commonality of experience on the level of depth theology. In Heschel's words, "theologies divide us, depth theology unites us." What unites Judaism and Christianity is the premise that there is a divine reality concerned with human destiny, that God demands something of us. "The crisis engulfs all of us. The misery and fear of alienation from God make Jew and Christian cry together."[79] The history and the destiny of Judaism and Christianity are interlocked, interrelated. *"No religion is an island.* We are all involved with one another. Spiritual betrayal on the part of one of us affects the faith of all of us."[80]

Significance for Jews

While Heschel advocated Christian commitment to the integrity of Jewish faith, he proclaimed the integrity of Christian faith to Jews. Not only did he make Jews aware of the marvelous spiritual resources of Christianity, but he taught that Christianity ought to be considered *preparatio messianica* by the Jewish community. A Jew "ought to acknowledge the eminent role and part of Christianity in God's desire for the redemption of all men."[81]

Heschel perceived a change in Christian attitudes towards Jews, and he conveyed that perception to Jews. Heschel said, "The attitude of the Christian community in America has undergone a radical change. Instead of hostility, there is respect and expectation, belief that Jews have a message to convey, significant insights which other people might share."[82] Heschel did not perceive this Christian change of view as a basis for Jewish self-complacency. Rather, he saw it as a challenge to the Jewish community. If non-Jews now perceive the Jewish soul to be pregnant with insights, Jews are required ever so much more to preserve their heritage, to cultivate their tradition, to seek religious self-understanding.

Heschel beseeched his fellow Jews to strive for spiritual authenticity. While other Jewish thinkers stress "Jewish survival," Heschel called for a Jewish revival. For Jews, Heschel insisted, the problem is not "to be or not to be," but "how to be, what to be." The Jewish quest must be for Jewish meaning, and not only for Jewish survival. The struggle for survival is a condition man has in common with animals. The quest for meaning is peculiarly human. "The significance of Judaism does not lie in its being conducive to the mere survival of a particular people but rather in its being a source of spiritual wealth, a source of meaning to all peoples."[83]

The world of Heschel's youth was destroyed by Hitler's horror. The Holocaust claimed the lives of his mother, his sisters, and six million of his Jewish brethren in Europe. Though Heschel has been criticized for having failed to allow the Holocaust to influence his thinking, such is not the case. Memory of the lost Atlantis of European Jewry was always with him. It was a motivating force behind his words and his deeds. More often implicit than explicit in his works, Heschel expressed his obsession with the lost continent of European Jewry. In *A Passion for Truth*, he wrote:

> Life in our times has been a nightmare for many of us, tranquility an interlude, happiness a fake. Who could breathe at a time when man was engaged in murdering the holy witness to God six million times?[84]
>
> We all died in Auschwitz, yet our faith survived. We knew that to repudiate God would be to continue the holocaust. We had once lived in a civilized world, rich in trust and expectation. Then we all died, were condemned to dwell in hell. Now we are living in hell. Our present life is our after-life. . . . [85]

When the first atomic bomb was dropped, Kerensky said that now the script of history has been changed. Similarly, for Heschel, after Auschwitz, after Hiroshima, philosophy and religion cannot be the same. In *Who Is Man?*, Heschel notes, "Philosophy cannot be the same after Auschwitz and Hiroshima. Certain assumptions about humanity have proved to be specious, have been smashed. What long has been regarded as commonplace has proved to be utopianism."[86] Similarly, in an address to religious educators, Heschel contended that, "Religion cannot be the same after Auschwitz and Hiroshima. Its teachings must be pondered not only in the halls of learning but also in the presence of inmates in extermination camps, and in the sight of the mushroom of a nuclear explosion."[87]

In confronting the Holocaust, in encountering the events of modern history, Heschel was no naive dreamer. He knew that evil exists, that the demonic persists. He knew that "the whole world [is] a burning bush, aflame with hatred, envy, and murder."[88] He knew that after the Holocaust there are no "final solutions," especially not theological ones. He maintained that "there is no answer to Auschwitz. To try to answer is to commit supreme blasphemy."[89]

In a speech to Christian theologians, Heschel responded to the response to World War II and to the Holocaust proposed by Dietrich Bonhoeffer and echoed by his disciples:

> The famous dictum of Dietrich Bonhoeffer "that a world that has come of age . . . could live without the tutelage" of God presupposes a view of our world which is, I believe, naive. Can you regard a world of Auschwitz and Hiroshima, of Vietnam and intercontinental ballistic missiles as a world that has come of age?[90]

For Heschel, our age has not "come of age." We live in an era of the "insecurity of freedom." Not security, but insecurity characterizes our existence. "What is the use of social security when you have a surplus of nuclear weapons?"[91] Heschel queries.

Heschel believed that though there can be no answer to Auschwitz, there must be a response, especially a Jewish response, to the Holocaust. For Heschel, that response is to have faith in God in spite of God, to realize that evil is a problem for man as well as for God. Anthropodicity—man's justification before God, is for Heschel, as significant if not more significant, than theodicy—God's justification to man. To the question of why the God of justice and compassion permits evil to exist, there can be no definitive answer. However, to the question of how man should aid God so that his justice and compassion might prevail, there is an answer—man can aid God by collaborating with him in the performance of sacred deeds, re-demptive deeds. In Heschel's words:

> This is the task: in the darkest night to be certain of the dawn,
> certain of the power to turn a curse into a blessing, agony into a
> song. To know the monster's rage and, in spite of it, proclaim to its
> face . . . ; to go through Hell and to continue to trust in the
> goodness of God—this is the challenge and the way.[92]

One cannot separate Heschel's social activism from his thoughts regarding the Holocaust. Indeed, it was as a response to the Holocaust that Heschel's social activism had such an air of special urgency. On one occasion, he noted,

> An ecumenical nightmare—Christians, Jews, Buddhists, dying to-
> gether, killing one another. So soon after Auschwitz, so soon after
> Hitler.
>   The question about Auschwitz to be asked is not: "Where was
> God?" but rather: "Where was man?"[93]

The Nazis claimed one-third of world Jewry and Heschel lived with the ghosts of those slain. He wrote, "Auschwitz is in our veins. It abides in the throbbing of our hearts. It burns our imagination. It trembles in our conscience."[94]

Heschel's greatest fear after the Holocaust was that Nazism might be able to claim a posthumous victory for having mur-dered Judaism as well as Jews, the Jewish soul as well as Jewish bodies. He therefore pleaded with and cajoled his fellow Jews not to officiate at their own spiritual self-annihilation. To one of his students, Heschel said, "When I think of what our people have accumulated over the centuries that nobody will ever know about, it seems like a second holocaust. Hitler destroyed our people. Now we let their spirit die." Thus, for Heschel, the primary imperative for Jews after the Holocaust is to rebuild their heritage, recapture their tradition, recreate their spirit, re-affirm their faith. Heschel's demand for Jewish religious self-understanding, his harsh criticism of the spiritual quality of contemporary Jewish life and institutions, was not an exercise in pomposity, but an urgent plea to halt the spiritual retardation of the contemporary Jewish soul, to stifle the suicide of the Jewish soul.

Heschel's life was a "passion for truth," a struggle for sincerity. His harsh critique of contemporary Jewish life drew few Jewish partisans to his banner during his lifetime. An institution in Jewish life himself, he posed too great of a threat to Jewish institutional life. He was rebuked by some Jewish leaders for his activities in civil rights, denounced by others for his repudiation of the war in Vietnam, and condemned by many for his opposition to Richard Nixon. But Heschel's quest was for integrity not popularity. He aspired to be an heir of the prophets rather than to become a modern celebrity. He preferred radical authenticity to institutionalized mediocrity. He opted for isolation rather than for self-deception. He perceived religious life as "spiritual effrontery" and "daily brinksmanship" rather than as cosmetic complacency. For being what he was, Heschel paid a price. During his lifetime he was never adequately appreciated by the Jewish community. He was ignored more than he was acclaimed; he was attacked more than he was appreciated. In all honesty it must be said that Christians appreciated his efforts more than Jews. His significance as a religious thinker, as a spiritual hero, was acknowledged by Christians long before it was perceived by Jews.

Heschel's significance for Jews is immense, but as of yet untapped. The legacy he left behind for Jews largely remains unknown. His spiritual and intellectual bequest to contemporary Jewry still awaits probate.

Notes

1. Hasidim are followers of Hasidism, a revivalist movement in Judaism which began in the eighteenth century.

2. Moses Maimonides was a leading medieval Jewish philosopher.

3. Saadya Gaon is often considered to be the "father" of medieval Jewish philosophy.

4. "Existence and Celebration," (New York: Council of Jewish Federations and Welfare Funds, 1965), p. 7.

5. "On Prayer," *Conservative Judaism* 25:1 (Fall 1970), p. 6.

6. *The Insecurity of Freedom* (henceforth: *IF*) (New York: Farrar, Straus and Giroux, 1966), p. 36.

7. "No Religion Is an Island," *Union Seminary Quarterly Review* 21:2 (January 1966), p. 117.

8. "Choose Life!," *Jubilee*, (January 1966), p. 39.

9. "The Moral Outrage of Vietnam," *Vietnam: Crisis of Conscience* (New York: Association Press, 1967), p. 50.

10. "Choose Life!," p. 39.

11. Letter dated October 20, 1972.

12. *The Earth Is the Lord's* (New York: Schuman, 1950), p. 106.

13. *The Quest for Certainty in Saadia's Philosophy* (New York: Feldheim, 1944), p. 1.

14. *A Passion for Truth* (henceforth: *PFT*) (New York: Farrar, Straus and Giroux, 1973), p. 107.

15. *The Earth Is the Lord's*, p. 83.

16. "A Conversation with Abraham Joshua Heschel" (henceforth: *Conversation*) (New York: National Broadcasting Co., 1973), p. 6.

17. *God in Search of Man* (henceforth: *GSM*) (New York: Harper, 1955), p. 8.

18. *GSM*, p. 19.

19. *Ibid.*, p. 102.

20. *Ibid.*

21. *IF*, p. 225.

22. "On Prayer," pp. 9–10.

23. In *The Synagogue School* 28:1 (Fall 1969), p. 19.

24. *IF*, p. 51.

25. *Ibid.*, p. 67.

26. *Ibid.*, p. 3.

27. *The Earth Is the Lord's*, p. 106.

28. *PFT*, p. 87.

29. *Ibid.*, p. 45.

30. *IF*, p. 125.

31. *Ibid.*, p. 119.

32. *Ibid.*, p. 136.

33. *Man Is Not Alone* (henceforth: *MNA*) (Philadelphia: Jewish Publication Society, 1951), pp. 143–4.

34. "The Mystical Element in Judaism" in *The Jews*, ed. Louis Finkelstein (Philadelphia: Jewish Publication Society, 1960), p. 951.

35. *Who Is Man?* (henceforth: *WM*) (Stanford: Stanford University Press, 1965), p. 22.

36. *Ibid.*, pp. 22–23.

37. *Ibid.*, p. 24.

38. *Ibid.*, p. 31.

39. *IF*, p. 158.

40. *Ibid.*, p. 152.

41. *Ibid.*

42. *GSM*, p. 189.

43. *Ibid.*, p. 188.

44. *The Prophets* (Philadelphia: Jewish Publication Society, 1962), p. 221.

45. *MNA* p. 241.

46. *WM*, p. 109.

47. *PFT*, p. 159.

48. *WM*, p. 111.

49. *IF*, p. 145.

50. *MNA*, p. 245.

51. *Israel: An Echo of Eternity* (henceforth: *Israel*) (New York: Farrar, Straus and Giroux, 1969), p. 224.

52. *PFT*, p. 191.

53. *MNA*, p. 92.

54. *Ibid.*, p. 166.

55. *Man's Quest for God* (henceforth: *MQG*) (New York: Scribner, 1954), p. 110.

56. *GSM*, p. 315.

57. *Ibid.*, p. 297.
58. *Ibid.*, p. 296; see *MQG*, p. 106.
59. *MQG*, p. 109.
60. *GSM*, p. 290.
61. *Ibid.*, p. 357.
62. *Ibid.*, p. 377.
63. *Ibid.*, p. 298.
64. *Ibid.*, p. 377.
65. *MQG*, p. 69.
66. "On Prayer," p. 2.
67. *MQG*, p. 70.
68. *Ibid.*, p. 78.
69. *Ibid.*, p. 10.
70. *Ibid.*, p. 19.
71. *Ibid.*, p. 12.
72. *GSM*, p. 36.
73. *Ibid.*, p. 243.
74. *IF*, p. 171.
75. "No Religion Is an Island," p. 124.
76. *Ibid.*, p. 129.
77. Reprinted in *IF*, pp. 168–79.
78. "No Religion Is an Island," p. 123.
79. *Ibid.*, p. 118.
80. *Ibid.*, p. 119.
81. *Ibid.*, p. 124.
82. "Existence and Celebration," p. 8.
83. *Ibid.*, p. 20.
84. *PFT*, pp. 300–301.
85. *Israel*, p. 112.
86. *WM*, p. 13.
87. "What We Might Do Together," *Religious Education* 62:2 (March-April, 1967), p. 134.
88. *Israel*, p. 132.
89. *Ibid.*, p. 115.
90. "The Jewish Notion of God and Christian Renewal," p. 116.
91. "What We Might Do Together," p. 134.
92. *PFT*, p. 301.
93. "What We Might Do Together," p. 134.
94. *Israel*, p. 206.